LANDMARK COLLECTOR'S LIBRARY

THE SPIRIT OF PARWICH

THE 20TH CENTURY IN PHOTOGRAPHS

Dr Isobel Combes

Published by

Landmark Publishing Ltd
Ashbourne Hall, Cokayne Ave, Ashbourne, Derbyshire DE6 1EJ England
Tel: (01335) 347349 Fax: (01335) 347303
e-mail: landmark@clara.net
web site: www.landmarkpublishing.co.uk

ISBN 1 84306 068 X

Print: Bookcraft, Midsomer Norton
Design: Mark Titterton
Cover: James Allsopp

Front cover: Early camping holiday.
It is not clear whether this wonderful car and caravan
was owned by a Parwich resident or whether the occupants are visiting.

Back cover top: Brentwood around 1900 before the shop was added.

Middle: Pantomime Cast 1987.

Bottom: The Oddfellows at Parwich Hall.

Title page: William Gosling (15) and his brother Robert (4) on William's bicycle.

LANDMARK COLLECTOR'S LIBRARY

THE SPIRIT OF
PARWICH

THE 20TH CENTURY IN PHOTOGRAPHS

Dr Isobel Combes

Landmark Publishing

CONTENTS

AUTHOR'S NOTE & ACKNOWLEDGEMENTS

Contributors

Patricia Bagshawe, John Booth, David Burford, William Bunting, Rosemary Chambers, Jack Cooper, Chris Duffell, Clem Edge, Brian and Dorothy Foden, Joyce Fortune (of photos belonging to Lizzie Ann Prince, born in Parwich in 1908), Elizabeth Frith, Len Gibbs, Cath Goldstraw, Carrie Gordon, Janet Gosling, Phyllis Gosling (photos scanned by Gill Radcliffe), Mike Goulden, Christopher Harrison, Ella Hopkinson, Denis Laycock, Peggy Lees, Barbara Lowes, Nigel Mace, Lu Matthews, John Myers, Alan and Violet Oldfield, Stella Porter, Mary Rawlins, Andrew Robinson, Margaret Rowan, Alice Shields, Donald and Rosemary Shields, Abel Shipley, Linda and Graham Taylor, Reg Twigge, Joyce and Ron Twigge, Gill Simpson, Anne Vidler David Wibberley and the Parwich WI (Scans by Gill Radcliffe). A number of photographs reproduced here are property of the Ashbourne News Telegraph and are included with their kind permission.

Thanks also to

Brian Foden, Peter Trewhitt, Sandra Chadfield, Abel Shipley, Mary Rawlins and Christopher Harrison for time spent helping to decipher photographs and identify people.

Special thanks to

Brian and Dorothy Foden and Peter Trewhitt of the Parwich and District Local History Society for their unfailingly generous help. Many of the photographs in this book come from Brian and Dorothy's extensive collection and their detailed knowledge of the village and its history have helped in the identification of many others. Peter's booklets, "Parwich Walks" (co authored with Patti Beasley) and "Gardening in Parwich" provided an invaluable resource and are frequently drawn upon in this book as are his articles in the Parwich and District Local History Society newsletter. A number of photographs reproduced here are property of the Ashbourne News Telegraph and are included with their kind permission.

INTRODUCTION

As I write this, the mist hangs low over the fields around Parwich, veiling everything beyond the nearby line of trees and enclosing the village in its own silent world. On such days, the village seems to have been here forever, taking shape out of the very rocks and earth beneath it.

Parwich is an ancient place. It is mentioned in the Domesday book in 1086 as Peverwic – probably translated as the dairy farm on the Pever, but the roots of the settlement go back much further, as evidenced by the ancient tombs of Minning Low which date back some 5000 years.

The Romans first valued the area for its lead mining and quarrying potential and this is where the first industry of Parwich lay, with major settlements at Lombard's Green and Roystone nearby. The latter became Roystone Grange, a monastic sheep farm. Although farming has always been a major part of the local economy, the surrounding quarries were even more significant for some time. Eventually, these came to take second place to the sheep and cattle farming which thrived on the rich grass and temperate weather. Crops, especially flax, were more important at an earlier time and the medieval ridge and furrow contours of many surrounding fields are still clearly visible when the sun is low in the sky.

As we enter the third millennium, rocked by so many disasters in agriculture, it remains to be seen where the economic focus of the area will turn. Even now, the Nestle factory in Ashbourne is in the process of closing and thereby depriving the area not only of its only large factory but of a major outlet for locally produced milk.

It is tourism and heritage which seem set to play an increasingly significant role now, with cyclists and walkers to be seen in all directions during the milder parts of the year, along with the caravanners and visitors.

Sadly, the last century has also seen a drastic decline in the internal economy and self sufficiency of Parwich – from three public houses, a number of shops, a post office, butcher's, garage and other local enterprises, we are down to one pub and one village shop. It is only through the heroic efforts of a number of people in the village that the latter has managed to survive at all. There was also, until recently, the train station at Alsop with services to Ashbourne and Buxton and even further afield on special occasions. Now the station is gone and the railway track turned over to footpaths.

However, it is important to remember that a place such as Parwich is not a collection of historical buildings and charming views, but a community of people. It is this community which has shaped this village over the centuries with people such as William Evans who acquired Parwich Hall in 1814 and financed the replacement of the Norman church with the present Victorian building. He also built the local school which is still in use and now being expanded. Fletcher Hampson came to be headmaster of this school and remained there until 1911 when he was succeeded by his son Fletcher Booth Hampson. The village bus shelter is adapted from the pump house that was erected in the memory of Fletcher Hampson to house the pump given to the village by James Brownson. James Brownson was a wealthy valuer and auctioneer whose family is descended from one Brownson (probably George) who came to settle in Parwich after serving as an attendant to Mary Queen of Scots during her imprisonment.

Some of our most vivid memories of Parwich life come from the writings of Helena Birkentall in the fifties of her experiences growing up in the village. She was the sister of Fletcher Booth Hampson and lived with him at Pool Croft, a house which was built for him on the site of the field where the Oddfellows used to meet, opposite the Crown Inn after which their Lodge is named. An equally fascinating visual history of Parwich has also come down to us thanks to the Gadsby sisters, of The Fold. These women were the nieces of William Greatorex, one of Parwich's great entrepreneurs, and were great postcard writers. These postcards have been collected and preserved and thus many images remain of the village in the early parts of the 20th century. It is astounding how much of it remains unchanged.

Over the century we see, in postcards and later in personal photographs, how the village participated in the events of the nation, celebrating the coronation of George V, serving in the wars, struggling though the snows of 1947 and acquiring such innovations as motorbikes and cars. The hospital on the hill was converted to a convalescent home for wounded soldiers, then later into a home for the elderly. In 1999, financial constraints forced the closure of the Home and it was sold into private hands. This closure reflects the gradual disappearance of village facilities over the century — in this respect as in many others, the great economic changes of the late twentieth and twenty-first century are almost inescapable.

Fortunately, Parwich is blessed with many who value its heritage and have sought to keep the best parts of it alive, both in the local organisations that keep up the old traditions and in the Local History Society which works to ensure that we do not lose touch with the past. While there is always a plentiful supply of scholars to record and discuss the event of great national importance, the history of the people themselves and their communities could vanish like today's mist were it not for those who remember, who treasure the old photographs of children dressed up for the Carnival, who can put names to the faces on the fading school photos, who can pass on their own memories of life growing up in Parwich.

To them all . . . thank you.

Above: "Parwich is a small and somewhat romantically situated hamlet, seven miles from Ashbourne" Derby Mercury 1873.

Right: Gibbons Bank.

Looking down into the village from Flatts Stile. This road leads into Parwich from the neighbouring village of Alsop-en-le-Dale, just outside of which was located the Alsop train station. This road is therefore called Station Road. In the background can be seen Parwich hill, at the top of which are the trees planted in the shape of a cross by the Revd Carr, (vicar of Parwich in the first part of the 19th century) to mark the accession of Queen Victoria to the throne.

Flatts Stile in 1915.

Entering Parwich. To the right can be seen the Methodist chapel which stands in an elevated position above the road.

Station Road, leading from Parwich to the train station (now closed) at Alsop-en-le-Dale.

The Methodist Chapel, built on Lenscliffe Rock in 1849, celebrating its 50th Anniversary.

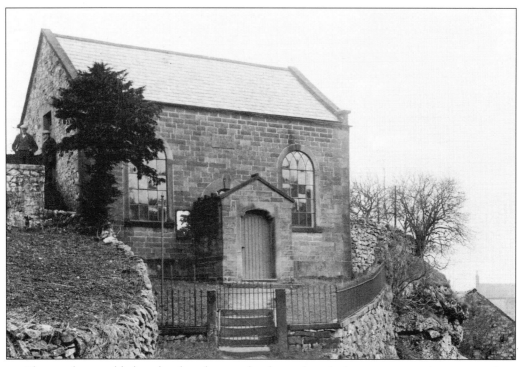

The porch was added to the chapel somewhat later, though there appears to be no record of the exact date.

The Fold. This house, perhaps one of the oldest in the village, has been put to a number of uses over the years: it has been a private school for girls, a guest house, the base of a carrier's business (the shed at the time being a hardware store) and, after the departure of the Misses Gadsby, it was the Parwich Working Men's Club until the mid 30s. It was also later occupied by Edward Halliday the artist, one of whose sketches hangs in the Memorial Hall.

The Fold.

Hallcliffe and the Village Green. This was, at one point, the home of Gerald Lewis who set up Parwich Creamery. It may also have served as the vicarage for a time. It and the Hall were the only private houses with running water at the time of the First World War.

Church Walk in the late 1920s. The building on the right is Church View, originally built as a pair of cottages but converted in the 1960s to a single house. It was the Post Office for some years, but has now been converted back to a pair of dwelling houses.

Flaxdale House, looking towards St Peter's Church. Flaxdale House was built in 1756 and was a farm until the twentieth century, later being converted to a youth hostel and then into a private home and B&B.

St Peter's Church was built in 1872 on the site of an older Norman church.

Japonica House, before it was extended by joining it to the cottage next door. The house belonged to the Swindell Family in the early 19th century as did many houses in that part of the village.

The Dam, when it was cleaned out. This was originally designed as the village sheep wash. According to the notes of Helen Birkentall, sheep washing time was in June, when hundreds of sheep were driven to the wash, watched by excited children out of school on their dinner hour. Later on, the sheep dip replaced the sheep wash and the Dam was left derelict until its conversion into a village pond.

The Sycamore Inn. Although there were once three pubs in the village (and possibly more, although their names and locations are now unknown), the Sycamore is the only one that remains in use.

Smithy Close in the 1980s. It was built as a collection of council flats and starter homes. It takes its name from the smithy that once stood on this site, opposite the Sycamore, and was demolished to make way for the Close. The buildings were completed in 1986.

Chestnut Cottages. It is an amusing oddity that the cottages on the same side of the road as the Sycamore are known as Chestnut cottages while the cottages on the opposite side are the Sycamore cottages. Chestnut cottages are named after the avenue of horse chestnuts that was planted further down the road to celebrate the Coronation of Queen Elizabeth II. Notice the car on the far right of the picture.

Nether Green, looking towards Nether Green House. The pond in this picture was drained quite some time ago and had been generally forgotten until the photo above came to light in 2002. As a result, the pond is now being restored, so this view has suddenly become more recognisable.

Nether Green House. Notice the monkey puzzle trees and the topiary for which there was once a bit of a craze in the village. The trees were probably planted between 1850 and 1860.

Nether Green. The green was grazed by cattle and other livestock up to the 1970s.

Westview Cottages around 1913. This photo was taken before the houses were inhabited – hence the paint on the windows and the rubble outside.

Creamery Road (or Lane) around 1912. The building on the left is Orchard View. Notice the motorcycle and wicker side car parked at the side of the road.

Creamery Road. In the centre of the photo can be seen Bob Steeples' petrol station. He had a couple of pumps here and ran a coach service taking workers to the cotton mill at Mayfield. He also provided a service into Derby for market day and into Ashbourne for the pictures on Saturday night. In addition to this he would pick up shopping for farmers and had a taxi which was driven by Ron Twigge.

The large house on the left was originally known as 'Off Creamery Road' until it was given the simpler title of 'The Croft'. Part of the building is now self contained and known as 'Tumbleweed'.

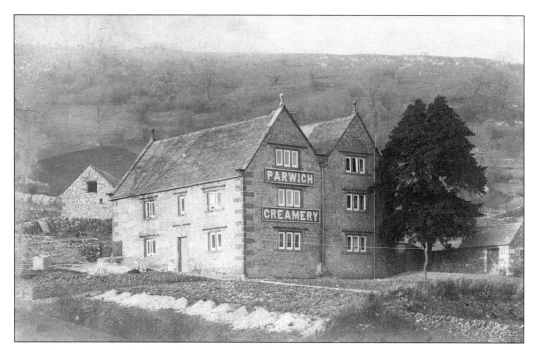

Parwich Creamery. The building dates from the 17th century and was converted to a cheese factory just after 1900 by Gerald Lewis – it supplied Parwich Dairy in Ashbourne. It was converted back to a private house in 1925.

Children outside Creamery Cottage in 1909, before the advent of the petrol pumps.

Gardener's Cottage. It came to be so called as it was used as the home for the gardener of the Hospital grounds, although it is in fact older than the Hospital itself. It was condemned and boarded up in the 1960s, but has been restored.

Originally built as the Rathborne Hospital, this building was later converted into a care centre for the elderly until demand for its services fell in the 1990s, forcing its closure. It is now a private residence.

Slaters Lane. To the right (beyond the photo) is the area where the market gardens were during the 1920s.

Gibbons Bank.

From above Pool Croft field, before the house was built. The field was the traditional starting point for the Oddfellows' Anniversary Parade. In 1938, Pool Croft house was built for Fletcher Booth Hampson, the headmaster at the village school and he lived here with his sister Helen Birkentall, whose notes of life in the village are an invaluable record of the time. During the Second World War, there were allotments here for the children.

The traditional association with the Oddfellows continues and they still stop at the house for refreshments during the parade.

Smithy Lane. On the left is Pool Croft, before the present driveway was added.

Elm Cottage, home to John Burford, Registrar of Births Marriages and Deaths. The Cottage was later demolished and the present vicarage was built on its site.

This arch by the front door of the vicarage is said to be part of Elm Cottage.

Building the present vicarage in 1917. It was considered a very modern and progressive building for its time and included elements, such as an office for the vicar separate from the domestic part of the building, which have only recently become compulsory in the design of today's vicarages. Fortunately, planning restrictions on new building in this area mean that this is one of the few large vicarages which have not yet been sold into private hands.

The present vicarage. The days when a village could expect to have its own vicar are long past, and Parwich is now part of a benefice of five parishes: Parwich, Alsop-en-le-Dale, Thorpe, Fenny Bentley and Tissington. Until the late 50s/60s, there were allotments for children on the hill behind the vicarage.

Crown Inn. Before this house became an inn, it may have been a base for a rope and sacking business. The sign for the Crown Inn can just be seen in this photo. The building is now a private residence.

Smithy Lane looking up towards Crown Cottage.

From the back of Close Farm, looking towards Rookery Cottage. There is evidence that this may have been a medieval farm site.

This aerial view of Close Farm was taken in the 1950s when it was still a working farm. It has since been converted into a private residence. The agricultural building to the top left of the picture has also changed substantially since then, having been converted to domestic use and incorporated into the next door cottage as Rookery House. It may once have been a timber framed, thatched building.

The Hall was built in 1747 by Sir Richard Levinge, on the site of an older (1550s) stone hall. To the left and closer to the Hall is the area which was turned over to allotments in the time of William Evans. Just visible at top left is part of the complex of buildings facing the Hall – Hall Coach House, the Stables and School View. It is here that William Evans built a schoolroom and facilities for a school master and his boarding pupils, before replacing that with the village school. The buildings later saw use as parish rooms and then as a reading room and chauffeur's flat. The Hall was later bought by Sir John and Lady Crompton-Inglefield in 1931 and then by the Shields family in 1976.

Parwich Hall with offices to one side. These were later replaced with a new wing designed by Sir Walter Tapper.

Looking down Pump Hill towards the one up one down house which was the home of the postman George Slater. It had been a saddler's and cobbler's shop before. There were no internal stairs in this house, so one had to go outside to get upstairs. The house was demolished sometime after 1950.

The Village Shop (left) has been trading since at least 1903, when the brick extension was built at a cost of £93. It was run as a grocer's and general store for many years by Mrs Wibberley, then Pam Slater followed by Larry Birds and, more recently, by Mike Goulden. It is now run by Emma Machin as a Spar franchise.

The village square, seen from Lenscliffe. On the left stands the village school.

Beyond the wall lie what were at one point the village allotments, probably set up by the Evans family in the 19th century and continuing so until 1930.

The original accommodation for the British Legion in Parwich. **From back:** George McCabe, Roy Lees, Angus Smith, Richard Knight, Fred Knight.

The new Legion building under construction. It was rebuilt from a derelict butcher/abattoir which was donated to the Legion by Sir John Crompton-Inglefield.

Building the Legion. **In background from left:** Roy Lees, Maurice Wheeldon, Fred Knight and Jack Skellern. **In foreground from left:** Brian Foden and Richard Knight. Here they are laying out the chatter which will be flattened to form the floor. Notice the outdoor toilets, still in use at the back.

Building the Legion. Brian Foden and Roy Millward working into the night to complete the gable end.

Col Peter Hilton, Lord Lieutenant of Derbyshire, opens the new Legion building in December 1989, by unveiling a brass plaque on which are inscribed the names of all those who had worked on the rebuilding and refurbishing. **From right:** Col Peter Hilton, J. Millward, F. Knight, R. Lees and J. Skellern.

November 1963. Sir Ian Walker-Okeover, Lord Lieutenant of Derbyshire, opens the Memorial Hall which was built to replace the old Institute building. Watching him are Sir John Crompton-Inglefield, the Revd F. Hansford, and the Revd P. L. Du Feu who was the Ashbourne Methodist Minister at the time. The Hall cost £6,000, of which £4,700 was raised by local events in the village itself.

Above and below: Reshingling the Memorial Hall. **Clockwise from front:** Fred Knight, George McCabe, Arnold Chadfield, Brian Foden, Andrew Knight, Roy Lees and Dennis Laycock. At the top centre of the photograph above can be seen Fernlea House, which is said to have been built by a Brownson (probably a George Brownson) who was one of the attendants of Mary, Queen of Scots and later came to settle in Parwich.

Brentwood, before the shop was added on for the Brownson family. Before the arrival of the Brownsons, the house was occupied by David Calladine who may be the man pictured here, although it might be Wright Greatorex of the Fold, who had a haulier's business.

Parwich Main Street.

The Hampson memorial housed the village pump and was built as a memorial to Mr Fletcher Hampson. The pump is now gone, and the structure serves as a bus shelter.

Parwich in the snow.

Sheffield University digging at Wigber Low outside Parwich. It is possible that bodies were once exposed on Wigber Low for the birds to pick clean before being buried on the nearby hill of Minning Low. Minning Low contains four 5,000 year old chambered tombs which were excavated in the 19th century and again in the 1970s but which have now been filled in. As its name suggests, Minning Low was associated with mining – in this case lead which would have been sought for by the Romans at nearby Royston, where a grange or sheep farm was established by a local monastery in the 13th – 14th century.

The School and School House were built in 1861 by Sir William Evans of Parwich Hall and it "was said at the time to be one of the finest village schools in the country" (H. Birkentall). It continued to be privately owned until it was sold to the local authority in 1918 by the Revd Claude Lewis who had made himself so unpopular by not allowing the village to use the building for the Coronation celebrations. The clock dates from 1865 and was built by Ellerby of Ashbourne. This photo was taken in around 1907.

Mr and Mrs Fletcher Hampson and the pupil teachers Miss Seals, Miss J.
Smith and Miss L. Hopkinson. Mr Hampson was headmaster of Parwich
School from 1870 to 1911.

Fletcher Booth Hampson, the son of Mr Hampson, succeeded his father as headmaster, continuing in that post for 38 years. He taught many of the present inhabitants of the village.

Lois Seals (née Hopkinson), one of the teachers at Parwich School.

Parwich School pupils around 1947. Back, from left: James Thomas, Douglas Allsopp, William Bunting, Gordon Edge, Mary Dale, Kenneth Biggs, Mary Brownlee, Joan Chadwick, Violet (?), June Tipper, Audrey Gibbs, Shelia Brownlee. **Second from back:** Geoffrey Twigge, Desmond Brownlee. Third from back: Elsie Weston, Alan Lowes, Malcolm Tipper, Kenneth Steeples, Brian Bradbury, Geoffrey Allsopp, Nigel Mace, Dennis Evans, Roy Lees, Ian Slater, ?, Charlie Fearn, Roy Ratcliffe, ?, Ian McConniche, Kathleen Steeples. **Third from back:** Mrs Yates, Reg Twigge, Lawrence Tipper, Marjorie Bradbury, Jane Edge, Mr Fletcher Booth Hampson, Keith Brownlee, Beryl Twigge, Doreen Lees, Veronica Twigge, Peter Ratcliffe, Mrs Lazarus, Sally Thomas. **Front:** ?, Malcolm Ratcliffe, Hazel Calladine, Marion Brownlee, Marjorie Walker, Pam Spencer, Shirley Alan, Terence Twigge, Phyllis Allsopp, Winston Blore, Lenny Chadwick.

Parwich School pupils.

Parwich School with Miss Yates.

Parwich School (from left) **Back Row:** ?, Don Wayne, ?, Ken Wayne, ?, ?. **Second from back:** Fred Brownlee, ?, Peggy Lees, ?, Phyllis Etches, Valerie Weston, Marjorie Twigge, Kate Shipley. **Third from back:** Mavis Edge, Barbara Mayers, ?, ?, ?, Betty Sims, ?, George Webster. **Front Row:** ?, ?, Cliff Sims, ?, ?, Ken Ward, ?

Parwich School. **Back Row from left:** Alfred Radcliffe, Eric Allsopp, Peter Adams, Harold Gibbs, Donald Lowndes, Derek Dale. **Second from back:** Donald Dale, Dorothy Goldstraw, ?, Joyce Twigge, Cath Steeples (Eileen Sonnex), Doreen Ryan, Jean Wibberley, Joyce Steeples. **Third from back:** ?, Lawrence Goldstraw, ?, Joyce Brownlee, Ernie Steeples, ?, Donald Allsopp. **Front:** Clarence Weston, Keith Sonnex, Albert Wilson, Derek Sonnex, Francis Allsopp.

Celebrating the School's Centenary 1861 – 1961. **Back Row from left:** Mrs Birch, Mr Fearn (Headmaster), Mrs Hansford, Mrs Leedham, Mrs Braddock, Mrs Dodds, Mr Hansford. **Second from back:** Janice Lees, Susanna Wayne, Caroline Fearn, Barry Kirkham. **Third:** Barry Wibberley, Susan Lees, Ann Webster, Glenys Wigley, Alan Hudson, Philip Webster, Chris Lowndes. **Fourth:** ?, Freda Webster, Janet Shipley, Sandra Wilton, Ruth Hudson, Roger Cundy, David Austen. **Front:** Lionel Webster, ?, Paul Allsopp, Kevin Goldstaw, Jane Twigge, Susan Webster, Susan Ridgard, Susan Johnson.

Mr Reed with the pupils of Parwich School.

At Parwich School c.1968.

Parwich School with Ada Birch and John Leslie Fearn. **The group includes:** Denise Johnson, Robert Bunting, Karen Steeples, John Birch, Janet Goldstraw, Michael Cundy, Joanna Bunting, Theresa Lees, Jeanette Oldfield, Tina Johnson, Wendy Bradbury, Robert Woolley, Debbie Gibbs, Elizabeth Bunting and Elizabeth Beech.

Parwich School Football Team 1925 – 26. **Back Row from left:** Fletcher Booth Hampson, Gordon Richardson, Les Chadwick, Harry Ward, Jack Richardson, Tommy Lees, Sid Wibberley, Frank Swindell. **Second row from back:** ?, ?, ?. **Front row:** Len Bradbury, Jack Sherrat, Abel Shipley, Norman Edge.

Parwich School Football team with Fletcher Booth Hampson
and the League Shield 1934 – 1935.

Parwich School Football Team in 1937 with the Cup and Senior Shield. **Back Row from left:** Jim Webster, Don Wayne, Mr Hampson, Ron Webster, Frank Gibbs, Billy Webster, Cyril Heathcote, Cecil Twigge. **Front Row:** Cyril Lowndes, Fred Brownlee, Bernard Wilson, Jack Hobson, Sam Wilson.

Parwich Football Team, 1954 – 55.

The opening of the school green. **From left:** Ray Williams (Headteacher), Paula Watson, Mark Bainbridge, Janet Bainbridge, Stuart Millward, Linda Taylor, ?, Marie Clarke, ?, Katie Harris, Ada Birch.

Children from the school singing "Listen to the Ocean" in one of Evelyn Weston and Elsie Webster's concerts to raise funds for the new village hall. Around 1960 – 61. **Clockwise from top left:** Glenys Wigley, Janet Shipley, ?, ?, Diane Twigge, Sandra Wilson.

Front from left: Barry Wibberley, Diane Twigge, ?, Anne Johnson, Paul Allsopp, Susan Webster, Susan Johnson, Susan Ridgard, Julie Brownlee, Sandra Wilton. **Second from front:** David Wibberley, David Lowndes, ?, Kevin Weston, Roger Cundy,?, Caroline Fearn, Moira Goldstraw, Glenys Wigley, Janice Lees. The woman at the back may be Doreen Lees.

Parwich Christmas Play. **Back, from left:** ?, Amy Danks, Rachel Tallis, Rachel Clews, Robert Taylor, David Gosling, Alan Hickmott, Stuart Hickmott, Paula Watson. **Second from back:** David Keeling, Daniel Flower, Jonathan Chadfield, Hayley Shaw, Thomas Keeling, Stuart Millward. **Third from back:** Andrew Wilton, Sam Beech, ?, ?. **Front:** Caroline Birds and Kimberley Shaw.

Parwich School performing Hansel and Gretel, Dec 2000.

Parwich School Revue, Dec 2000. **Back, from left:** Rob Francis, Stuart Millward, Margaret Lees, Dorothy Foden, Carol Cooper, Laura Chadfield, Val Charlton, Carl Wilton, Natalie Lowndes, Brian McCormick. **Front, from left:** Catherine Eaton, Helen Swindell, Becky Wood, Caroline Birds.

Chapter 3 – St Peter's Church

St Peter's Church Parwich. The present church was built, at the expense of William Evans, by Robinson of Derby at a cost of £4,500 in 1872. It replaced an older church which had stood on the same site.

The original St Peter's Church. It was criticised in the 19th century for being too small, ugly and clumsy in design. Its replacement with a newer building, however, did not meet with universal approval in the village – "Where is now the low, ivy covered square tower, through which one entered and saw the sexton toll the bell? Where is the sculptured sword, thought to be crusaders? Where the pulpit for the Parson with the desk under it for the clerk? Where the choir with its diverse instruments of music in the gallery? Where the square pews that belonged to the several farms and gave a special and personal interest to the occupants? All gone! All swept away to satisfy the ritualistic fancies of a sacerdotal parson. Thus is England being spoiled of its glory. (Notes by Joseph Thompson of Parwich 1833-1909). The Ashbourne Telegraph of the 5th July 1895, refers to documents from 1701, detailing the payment of a shilling for ale for the workers when the church leads were laid (this would have bought about 6 pints).

This photo was taken in the early 1900s. In 1919 a carillon was added in memory of those who died in the First World War. It bears a plaque that reads "To the glory of God, to commemorate the victory won in the Great War of 1914 – 19 and in proud and grateful memory of those men of Parwich who fought and died, this Carillon of eight bells of memory was installed in the year of our Lord 1919 by Alfred John Gainsford, Major R.F.A., T.F. and Joint Lord of the Manor of Parwich and Edith Geraldine his wife." The carillon is still in use to this day.

Notice the yew tree in the churchyard. The Parwich Church Wardens' Accounts for 1713, refer to the planting of yew trees in the churchyard at a cost of 3 shillings and 6 pence, including fetching and another 6 pence for setting it. 5 shillings were paid to Millward and John Yates to rail it about and 5 shillings for the wood needed to do so. In comparison, the Church Warden's wage for that year was 4 shillings. The 1713 Church Warden's Account is the only one that seems to have survived from this period for Parwich Church. The rest may have been lost when the church was rebuilt in 1872. (The full version of the Account is published in an article by Brian Foden in the 1999 parish magazine. The original Account is available at the records office in Matlock).

From the past: Elements of the original Norman building were incorporated into the new structure, most importantly this Tympanum now over the west door. This is older even than the Norman church as it seems to date from around 700 – 1100 and may have been part of an earlier Saxon church. It has deteriorated considerably since this photo was taken, due to modern day pollution.

To the future: This window is one of two in the Lady Chapel that were commissioned to celebrate the Millennium. In their panes are engraved the names of every child in the village who was under the age of 14 at the end of 1999. The windows were designed by David Pilkington of Chapel-en-le-Frith and made by Illumin Stained Glass of Macclesfield.

The Parish Chest. This is the lid of the church's 17th century parish chest. Stored under the church in the boiler room, it was recovered in 1993, by which time only the lid could be salvaged.

"I used to see two oak chests in the chancel and wondered what they contained. It was said the candles for lighting the church were stored there because the mice played havoc with them when they were stored in the cupboards on the wall. I used to see one, bolder than the rest, from my perch in the gallery. It used to run out of its hole and take a nibble from the candlestick placed in its holder ready. But it must have satisfied the hunger of the poor thing that looked as small and famished as any church mouse must do!" (John Thompson).

The condition of the chest when it was recovered from the storage area under the church by Jack Cooper and Denis Laycock in 1993. It had been severely damaged by the damp.

The Interior of St Peter's around 1906. Notice the stone pulpit which was replaced with a wooden one after 1907.

Interior of St Peter's. The screen, designed by Sir Walter Tapper, was added in 1907.

Above: The Revd Leighton Buckwell – standing second from the left. Leighton's father, the Revd William Buckwell sits at the far left, and Leighton's brother William, also a clergyman, stands second from the right. They are surrounded by their wives and children. In 1872, according to Helen Birkentall, the Revd Buckwell wrote in the annual parish magazine: "We must restore the present Norman church or build a new one". He must have been a determined man – a faculty was granted in 1873 to demolish the Norman church and to start work on the new building.

Right: Christopher Harrison, the present vicar of Parwich, came to the parish in November 1996. He is also vicar of Alsop-en-le-Dale, Fenny Bentley, Thorpe and Tissington.

Left: The Revd Victor Brown at his farewell party. From left: Hugh Gibson, Joan Brown, Victor Brown, Denis Laycock, Doreen Jameson-Booth, William Bunting and Clem Edge.

Above left and right: A Christmas Flower Festival in 1986 to raise funds for the repair of the church organ. Parwich has a long tradition of skilful flower arranging and the St Peter's church is always magnificently decked out on special occasions.

Setting up a train in the grounds of Parwich Hall for the 1998 Church Fete.

From left: Dorothy Foden, Betty Fentern, Jack Cooper, Janet Gosling, Mrs Buck, Mrs McShane.

Church Fete. **Back, from left:** Mrs Wheeldon, Cliff Goldstraw, Val Kirkham, Marjorie Bunting.
Front: Janet Gosling, Sam Beech(?), Caroline Birds, ?.

Church Fete in 1992. **At back:** Julie Goodwin, Debbie Webster, Trevor Webster.
At front: Alison Cooper, Elizabeth Ryder, Amanda Pickard.

Margaret Lees and Mr Read at a Church fete held at Close Farm.

Sunday School Nativity play, around 1990. **Adults, clockwise from lower left:** Debbie Webster, Val Kirkham, Ann Cooper. **Children include:** Nicholas Birds, Stuart Hickmott, Laura Chadfield, James Taylor, Philip Kirkham, Jonathan Chadfield, Adam Swindell, Helen Swindell, Laura Wood, Penny Harris, Lisa Wood, Simon Wood and Rebecca Wood.

Florence Ada Monica Rathborne was the daughter of the Revd. Rowland German Buckaton of Bradbourne. Before Florence's death in 1900, she asked her husband to use the proceeds from the sale of her property to endow a convalescent home for women and children. Her husband, Ambrose, died before he could put her wishes into effect, but had ensured that Florence's wishes were included in his own will. A trust was set up to finance the hospital and a site in Parwich was chosen. The building of the Hospital started in 1911 and the Hospital was ready in 1914. During the First World War, it was used by the British Red Cross as a convalescent home for wounded soldiers. In 1940, Mrs Leonard Hardy of Alsop-en-le-Dale (who later became Mrs C. Boyd), was given the task of restarting the hospital, and it was reopened on 10th February 1941 by the Dowager Duchess of Devonshire who was then the President of the Derbyshire Red Cross. During the Second World War, it again treated wounded servicemen. In 1948 the building was acquired by the N.H.S. (for £1.00!) and continued as Parwich Hospital until its closure in 1979. A local trust was formed to purchase the building in 1981 for conversion into a nursing home, known as the Care Centre, for the elderly. The Hartington GP practice also held a bi-weekly surgery here for patients in the village.

In the late 1990's, a decline in demand for places at the Home led to its closure and the building is now a private dwelling.

Left: The interior of the Hospital during its time as the Rathborne Convalescent Home. Rosemary Meynell, who visited Parwich in the early 1950s, wrote that the hospital was more like a home than an institution as it lacked the "intimidating white starchiness associated with hospitals".

Above: This is said to be the Princess Royal during her visit to the Rathborne Hospital in 1944. However, other photographs of the Princess' visit (p.66) show her to be wearing a different uniform. This would indicate that the woman above is not the Princess or that she visited the village twice during the war. A local newspaper, the Express and Star, records that the Princess visited an auxiliary hospital and a Red Cross Hospital in the Midlands in 1941. It is possible that it was the Rathborne Hospital she came to and that these two photographs were taken then.
Left: Here she is shaking hands with Ted Halliday, the artist, who served in the Home Guard at Parwich.

Mrs Hardy, Commandant of the Derby 72 Red Cross, with the staff of the Rathborne Hospital, shortly after its opening in 1941. **Front, from left:** ?, Ruth Russell, Betty Sampson, Mrs Hardy, Dr Hollick, Matron Badger. **Back, from left:** ?, Margaret Adams, ?, Dorothy Falder, ?, ?, Margaret Woodward, Theresa Woolley (the ambulance driver), ?, ?, Mrs Handley, Ruth Buxton.

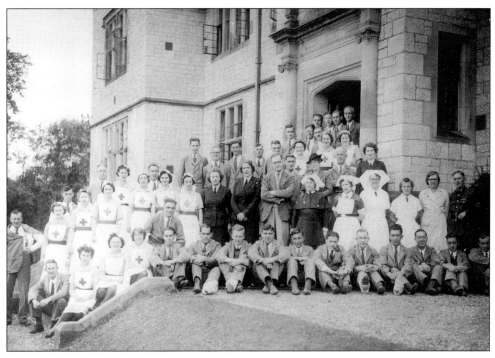

Mrs Hardy with the staff and patients. There were only 34 beds at the beginning, most of which were mattresses, as the beds had been bombed in Birmingham! Eventually, though, Mrs Hardy and her colleagues bought and borrowed enough equipment to accommodate up to 98 patients. Over 4,000 cases were cared for during the Second World War.

The visit of the Princess Royal (Princess Mary) to the Care Centre on September 21st 1944. **Front, from left:** Matron Wysall, ?, Mrs Hardy with her granddaughter Susan Stephenson, The Princess Royal, The Dowager Duchess of Devonshire, Mr Pulvertaft, Dr Hollick. **Second row:** Kathleen Sayles, Margaret Adams, Beryl Poole, Sister Price, Margaret Woodward, Theresa Woolley, Sister Mason, Joan Fletcher Shaw, Evelyn Land, Lillian Lawrence, Miss Mills. **Third row:** ?, Jean Ivers (a Land Girl from the Channel Islands who took care of the gardens and grounds of the Hospital), ?, Patricia Hall, Letty Sampson, Doreen Ginnis, Staff Sergeant Shipp. **Back row:** Mary Robinson, Francis Scott Owen, Nancy Parker, Dorothy Falser, Ruth Russell, Mrs Hobson, Joyce Steeples, Staff Sergeant Hussey.

The Princess Royal with the patients at the Hospital. Joyce Steeples (now Twigge) remembers that the convalescing soldiers could get a little too lively, in spite of the sergeants in charge of them. On one occasion, she remembers, they went on the rampage and broke out of the hospital to go down to the Sycamore pub. The next morning the culprits were lined up along the corridor and packed off to the army hospital at Catterick in Yorkshire.

A visit by the Duchess of Kent. **Front row, from left:** Matron Wysall, Mr Pulvertaft, Mrs Hardy, The Duchess of Kent, The Dowager Duchess of Devonshire, Theresa Woolley (the ambulance driver), Dr Hollick. The nurses who did not come from the village itself were housed at Hallcliffe House and then later at Fearnlea House.

The Duchess of Kent meeting the nurses and kitchen workers. To the back, from the right are Jo McConnichie, Eva Lees, Jessie Weston. **From right:** Olive Hobson, Mrs Handley, Joyce Steeples (now Twigge), Evelyn Land.

The Care Centre minibus was donated by Stanley Thornton, on the left beside Lady Caroline Waterhouse. Also in the photo are Ron Birch, Evelyn Land, Ida Bradbury, Mrs Harris and Colin Chadwick.

Ida Bradbury (who did not use a wheelchair!) demonstrating the lift on the bus. **From left:** ?, Mrs Harris, Mr Barnes, Ron Birch, Stanley Thornton, Ida Bradbury, Lady Caroline Waterhouse, Donald Shields.

A drink at the Care Centre. **From left:** Esther Flower, Ida Bradbury, Ella Hopkinson.

The Duke of Devonshire visits the Care Centre. **Seated at the front, from left:** Ella Hopkinson, Ray Stone, Betty Stone.

Chapter 5 – The Local Economy

Parwich Village had at one time a thriving local economy which has, sadly, almost vanished. The 1841 census records the presence of a joiner's shop, a grocer's shop, a butcher, a tailor, a dressmaker, a saddler, a blacksmith, two schools and three pubs: the Sycamore, the Wheatsheaf and the Crown Inn (of these only the Sycamore survives).

The census also records 30 farmers, 44 farm labourers, 7 sawyers, 4 weavers, 3 masons and 3 shoemakers as resident in the village.

Webster's Shop.

The Crown Inn, kept by John Prince in the early 1900s. The woman talking to the carter is his wife Annie Prince (née Hadfield). She was not very happy about the photo having been taken as she was still wearing her pinafore from blackleading the grate.

Annie was born in Parwich in 1871 and married John Prince in 1893, becoming stepmother to his two children by his first wife. They left the Crown in 1915.

The Wheatsheaf was another of the pubs in Parwich. Little is known about it and it has now been divided into two private dwellings.

The Sycamore dates back to the 17th century.

Janet Gosling is the present landlady of the Sycamore, having taken over in 2000 from Don Keyworth who ran the pub for 13 years. Here she receives her certificate to become a Frederic Robinson licensee, from Robinson's director Dennis Robinson.

Brentwood was converted for George and Esther Brownson to run as one of the village's shops. The shop itself was run by Esther and her sister in law Anne, while George kept up a frame manufacturing business in a workshop behind the house.

Wright Greatorex at the Fold. He started out as a groom and gardener at the Hall, but proved to be one of the village's most energetic and ambitious businessmen. He eventually ran, among other things, a carrier's business, an ironmonger's and a guesthouse at the Fold for up to 24 guests.

The Village Green with Wright Greatorex's shop to the right. The sign reads "Wright Greatorex Draper, Boot and Shoe Dealer. Motor Car for hire. Enquire at the house."

The Fold.

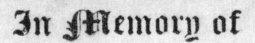

In Memory of

THE LATE

THOMAS GIBBS.

———

Therefore be ye also ready;
for in such an hour as ye think
not the Son of man cometh.

Matthew, c. 24, v. 44.

———

HANNAH IRONMONGER,

Funeral Biscuit Baker, Parwich.

— —

W. HOON, TYP ASHBOURN.

Hannah Ironmonger, the baker of the funeral biscuits, lived in a house opposite the Pinfold, near where the Chapel was later built. Funeral biscuits appear to have been a custom prevalent in this area, Yorkshire and the East Coast of America in the 19th century. According to Jack Cooper, onetime vicar of Parwich "The practice of making funeral biscuits is in fact a Staffordshire custom and were long, thin finger biscuits. The custom was to give the men a clay pipe and half an ounce of tobacco and the ladies a funeral biscuit . . . funeral biscuits and clay pipes were particularly common around the Warslow area." (J. Cooper, Parwich & Alsop Church Magazine, January 1994). Nothing else is known about Hannah Ironmonger's funeral biscuit baking business, but White's 1857 Directory of Derbyshire mentions her husband Benjamin Ironmonger as a confectioner in Parwich, though in the 1851 Census he is listed as an agricultural labourer.

The Cottage on the Green and Ivy Cottage. In the 1850s, one of these houses was a private school, the Green in front serving as a playground, hence the stone stoups – a boy is perching on one of these at the far left of the photograph.

The Village Post Office around 1909. In the centre of the group is George Shaw the one armed postman.

The Post Office. There is, sadly, no longer a Post Office in Parwich.

Mary Graham who ran the Post Office until the late 1980s.

Retirement of Mary Graham, the Parwich postmistress, in 1984. She had been postmistress since 1954, succeeding her mother who became postmistress shortly after the family came to Parwich from Co. Durham in 1914. One of Mary Graham's first jobs was to deliver the mail for the Parwich area – which required a daily 16 mile round trip by bicycle. **From left :** Donald Shields, Dorothy Foden, Ella Hopkinson, Esther Flower, Cath Goldstraw, Enid Edge, Valerie Flower.

Harry Twigge delivering the milk, with Tommy the horse. Before Harry acquired the cart, he used to deliver the milk in an even more traditional manner – from buckets suspended from yoke across his shoulders!

Above: For many years, Mike Goulden ran Parwich shop and at his retirement there was a danger that the shop would have to close and be sold for residential use. However, thanks to a substantial financial investment on the part of the village, the shop has been able to continue in business and has recently been converted to a Spar outlet which will give it the support and advantages of being associated with a national brand.

Right: Mike and Fly.

Emma Machin, who now runs Parwich Shop.

The derelict smithy opposite the Sycamore. It was one of the two smithies in Parwich and was pulled down in 1970 to allow Smithy Close to be built.

"One of the most memorable sights of my early life was the procession of farm horses from the smithy to their respective homes. They were in most cases brought down under escort, but the return journey was very different. The escort returned to the farm, and after shoeing, the blacksmith slapped the leader on the back and away they all trotted to Hawkslow, Low Moor, Hill-Top and so on. No loss or accident ever came to my knowledge." H. Birkentall.

The second smithy was on Smithy lane and faced Elm Cottage, where the present vicarage would be built. It, too, became derelict and was rebuilt as a private home.

Alsop Moor Works during the snow of 1947. Alsop Moor Works of I.C.I. (Lime) Ltd, with its 200 ft Hoffman Kiln chimney was closed in 1949 and demolished in September 1952.

The same view today.

Above and opposite page: The limestone quarry at Ballidon, just outside the village, is now run by Tarmac Central Ltd and produces industrial powders and fillers for markets throughout the UK as well as calcium carbonate granules for use in the production of agricultural feedstuffs and fertilisers. It also plays a part in the preservation of local history by sponsoring the production of the Parwich and District Local History Society Newsletter.

Bradbourne Mill lies on the very edge of the parish boundaries. Parts of its timberwork date back to medieval times. Although there are records of there having been a mill in Parwich itself, no traces of it have yet been found.

Phyllis Webster on the Whitecliffe Farm tractor during World War II.

Haymaking. Parwich logbooks from the past frequently record children as being absent from school for haymaking and harvesting.

Haymaking. The school tower can be seen in the background.

Upper Moor farm in the 1950s. In the late 1940s, a reservoir was built at the farm to supply mains water to Upper Moor and the surrounding farms. Mains electricity did not arrive until the 1960s and there was no telephone until the 1970s (though the dog Spot was well trained to carry notes from Upper Moor Farm to Lower Moor Farm). Milking was still done by hand until the 1950s when an oil driven milking machine arrived.

George Keeling and friend on the hay dray – loading the hay.

Upper Moor Farm. George Keeling and Jeff Bestwick with a young shire horse. The car lurks in the background, an ominous shadow of things to come.

George Critchlow with his horse drawn hay rake and passengers!

Mary Rawlins with a friend at Upper Moor Farm.

Dinah (the horse) with Phyllis (Peggy) Webster. Taken in the 1950s.

James (Jim) and William Webster (left and right) to the left of the binding machine at Whitecliffe Farm.

Another load of hay heads for the barn at Whitecliffe Farm. Behind the haycart is the farm's hay loader, which saved a significant amount of manual work.

Whitecliffe farm wedding.

George Shaw with Bonny at Parwich Lees.

Ray Kirkham, Biff and Poyce haymaking at Parwich Lees.

Above: Foufinside Farm
c.1962. The Gosling family
moved to the farm in 1973.

Right: William Gosling at
Hilltop Farm.

William Gosling, dry stone walling - an important skill in this area.

James Bunting at Low Moor Farm in 1989, with some unusual twins. The Friesian cow had managed to give birth to two calves with different fathers – one Friesian, the other Limousin.

Cliff Goldstraw with cows. Crops were once grown around Parwich, and the raising of pigs – to judge from the number of old pigsties in the village – was once an important activity. However, farming in this area now centres almost entirely on sheep and dairy cattle.

Wakes week in 1920s. As older residents of the village often point out, the relative isolation of Parwich means that people here have developed a tradition of providing their own entertainment and of strong community feeling. Village events have always been well supported in the past, and generally continue to be so despite the growing encroachments of today's long working hours and electronic entertainment.

Celebrating the opening of the Memorial Hall. **From left:** Stan Weston, Betty Weston, Kathleen Allsopp, Mrs Nadin, Ella Hopkinson.

Roystone Rocks, Church Outing.

Outside the Institute (which was later replaced by the Memorial Hall) in the 1930s.
Possibly the cast of the village pantomime.

Wakes Week Carnival. **Clockwise from lower left:** Brian McCormick, Jane Harris, Roger Cundy, Joan Millward, Arnold Chadfield, Roy Millward, Peter Harris.

Wakes Week Carnival Morris Dancers. **Back row from left:** Margaret Lees, Carol Cooper, Edith Ryder, Pauline Laycock, Karen Watson, Edwina Flower, Ann Wheeldon, ?,?, Belinda Lowes. **Front:** Flo Harris, Dawn Allsopp, Evelyn Shaw, Jean Wayne.

Outside the old Post Office. Wakes Week Carnival has always included a number of themed floats.

The children showing off their costumes in the 1940s This is another
traditional element of Wakes Week.

Left: Early 1960s entry to the Carnival from Parwich Lees with Michael Kirkham on top of the cab.

Below: **Patient:** Monica Edge, **Nurses:** Caroline and Robin Kirkham, **Surgeon:** Pamela Kirkham.

David Wibberley in the Carnival, 1960s.

The Wombles! Carnival 1974.

Robin Hood and his Merry Men Float.

Carnival 2001. Charlotte and Sophie Phillips (granddaughters of Anne and Fred Knight) visiting Parwich for the Carnival.

Maypole Dancing. This is said to have been taken in Parwich, perhaps in Cuckoo Lane. Could it be that this is part of the Whit Week Sunday School procession, as recorded by Helen Birkentall, when every girl would wear a white dress with a coloured silk sash and matching hair ribbon for the occasion?

The Parwich Imps Jazz Band 1935.

Concert by Parwich Ladies, 1960. **From left:** Cath Goldstraw, Peggy Lees, Joyce Twigge, Elsie Webster, Evelyn Weston.

"The Pipers of Parwich" in front of Dodds Hill at Ball Croft. **Back, from left:** Betty Weston, Mrs Webster, Annie Wibberley, Evelyn Weston. **Front, from left:** Elsie Webster, Barry Wibberley, Connie Edge.

Left: Pantomime Cast. **Clockwise from lower left:** Stephen Hart, Janice Wigley, David Woolley, Angus Smith, Alison Meadows, Rob Francis, Roy Millward, Denis Laycock, Delia Wayne.

Below: Pantomime Cast 1987. **Clockwise from lower left:** Debbie Meadows, Dorothy Foden, Roy Lees, Rosemary Chambers, David Woolley, Sue Carver, Angus Smith, Janice Wigley, Roy Millward, Denis Laycock, Peter Harris, Ron Birch, Brian McCormick, Gill Simpson, Joanne Black, Edith Rider, Pam Meadows.

Pancake Race, 1991. **From left:** Anne Beach, Wendy Birds, Christine Duffell, Rosemary Dunn, Ray Williams (Headteacher, Parwich School).

Egg and Spoon Race.

Chapter 8 – Groups and Societies

For such a small village, Parwich has a strong tradition of groups and organisations. One of the oldest of these is the Loyal Laurel and Crown Lodge of Oddfellows, pictured above, in about 1914, on their annual walk to the church at the beginning of Wakes week. In addition to the Oddfellows, to which almost every man in the village belongs, there is a wider range of groups in the village, catering to a multitude of interests from the Under Fives Club to the British Legion and the Women's Institute. Some are still vigorously supported, others have vanished, like the Women's Club whose counterpart to the Oddfellows walk used occur on Whit-Monday, the day after the Sunday School procession. Fortunately other groups, such as the recently revived Youth Group, continue to come into existence, thereby keeping up the traditions of community involvement and reflecting the changing interests of the times.

The Parwich and District Horticultural Society was founded in 1952 and reflects the great interest in gardening to be found in Parwich. **Back row from left:** Mr Rich, Edgar Adams, Eric Allsopp, Barry Forton, Abel Shipley. **Front row:** Kathleen Allsopp, Betty Weston, Chief of Derby Parks.

Parwich Horticultural Society Show in the 1970s. **Back, from left:** Eric Allsopp, Roger Garside, Ambrose Wilton, Nick Canter, Arthur Wayne. **Middle, from left:** ?, Brian Foden, Abel Shipley, John Worthington. **Front:** ?, Dorothy Foden.

Parwich Horticultural Society Show 1990. **Back, from left:** Abel Shipley, Charlie Fearn.
Front: Dorothy and Brian Foden.

Bob Matthews, chairman of the Horticultural Society at the annual show in 1999. Bob was a popular
member of the village community and his funeral in 2002 packed St Peter's Church.

The committee of the Parwich and District Local History Society at their Christmas party in 2002. Left to right is Mike Goulden, Rob Francis and Peter Trewhitt. The Local History society was formed in 2000 after a series of local history lectures sparked enthusiasm for the subject. It publishes a monthly newsletter and various booklets, maintains a website and holds regular meetings and lectures. In 2002, it held a series of exhibitions and talks to mark the Queen's Jubilee.

Brian Foden and Andrew Robinson, members of the Parwich and District Local History Society, launching their booklet on the history of St Peter's Church, Parwich.

Left: Nia Linnell in the British Legion Parade, when the standard flag was changed from The Parwich British Legion to The Royal Parwich British Legion.

Below: **From left:** Lady Hilton, Donald Shields, Nia Linnell.

Parwich WI winners of the 1982 Women's Institute Drama Festival. **Back from left:** Patti Beasley, Virginia Buchanan, Ann Wheeldon. **Front:** Barbara McCormick, Dorothy Foden, Rosemary Chambers.

Women's Institute. Teaparties Anywhere Event, 1990. **Back, from left:** John Fuller-Sessions, Dorothy Littlewood, ?, Marion Fuller-Sessions, Rosemary Chambers, Pat Wright, Ann Brown, Ann McCabe. **Front:** Dorothy Foden, Anne Knight.

Left: The Parwich Over 1960's club was formed in 1974 to organise social events for the older members of the village, such as this visit to Stratford in the mid 1980s.

Left: Parwich Under Fives, (known as the Mother and Baby Group until 1994) enjoy their Christmas Party, with John Lees as Father Christmas.

Right: Parwich Under Fives in the Village Hall.

Parwich Under Fives Christmas 2000.

Seth Amos and Lucy Dale at the Stepping Stones Pre-School teddy bears picnic in 2001. The Stepping Stones Pre-School (based in the Memorial Hall) was originally the Brassington Playgroup and came to Parwich in 1998 after becoming a validated pre-school.

At one time there were both Girl Guides and Brownies in Parwich. Sadly, this is no longer the case. **Back row from left:** Janet Gosling, Eileen Burns, Dorothy Foden, Helen Wheeldon, Cassie Beasley, Olivia Flower. **Middle:** Katy Dunn, Emily Twigge, Philippa Harris, Naomi Millward, Penny Harris, Hannah Lowe. **Front:** Rachel Tallis, ?

Parwich Girl Guides. **From left:** Laura Chadfield, Amanda Pickard, Paula Watson, Katie Harris, Julie Duffell.

Parwich Boy Scouts. On the right is Ronnie Calladine, great-grandson of David Calladine who was at Brentwood before the Brownsons.

The Loyal Laurel and Crown Lodge of Oddfellows dates from 1836 and was originally based at the Crown Inn on Smithy Lane. The Oddfellows movement originated as a substitute trade organisation in areas where the population was too small to support dedicated guilds. The aims of the association were, among others, to provide for members, or their widows and orphans, in times of need.

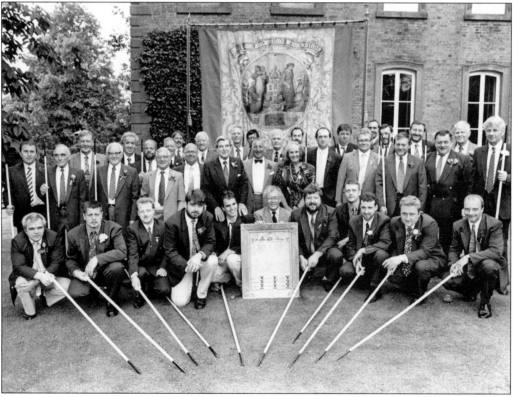

The Oddfellows at Parwich Hall, with the white wands which are carried in their annual parade around the village and which appear to be unique to the Parwich Lodge. They are first mentioned in the records in 1845. At the centre can be seen the Dispensation, the handwritten document giving permission for the founding of the Lodge. This is carried at the head of every Anniversary Parade.

Above: The Oddfellows Anniversary Celebration, consisting of a parade with a band, followed by a dinner, is held every year on the Monday closest to the 29th of June (the patronal festival of St Peter's Church). This event marks the beginning of the Parwich Wakes – a week of entertainments including a sports day and a fancy dress carnival.

Left: Outside Wayne's shop with the banner which is carried in every parade and probably dates from 1847. **From left:** Tom Lees, Vernon Wibberley, ?, Ron Twigge, Len Gibbs.

Above and below: The Oddfellows. Notice that in these two photographs there is no sign of the Dispensation which is usually carried at the head of the Oddfellows parade. This may indicate that what is shown here is not in fact the Oddfellows Anniversary Walk as has been thought, but some other village celebration. Helen Birkentall records that on occasions of great national importance, such as a Jubilee or Coronation, there would be "a procession which included every phase of village folk. Starting from the School Green, they marched to church with flags attached to each section, also a band and a banner preceding the Odd – Fellows, to finish what must have been a very colourful, impressive sight." Notice also the woman on the left in the lower photograph, in the long black skirt and large hat. She also appears on the photograph of the coronation celebration seen on p.169.

The Oddfellows at Parwich Hall.

Parwich Oddfellows Anniversary Dinner held in the Sycamore Inn Club Room in the 1950s.
Standing: Trustee Albert Berresford. **At the top table:** Sir John Crompton-Inglefield, Revd Hansford, John Leslie Fearn (School Headmaster) **Also shown:** Tom Hall, Les Chadwick, Cecil Twigge, Abel Shipley, Tom Kinder, Walter Wilson, Reg Twigge.

From left: Denis Laycock, ?, Debbie Webster, Trevor Webster and Angus Smith campaigning for the hard pitch area which now provides footing for the Parwich Tennis Courts.

Parwich Football Team. **Back Row from left:** D. Rowe, Len Gibbs, Don Wayne, Abel Shipley, J. Harrison, Fred Brindley, G. Tipper. **Front row:** Fred Brownlee, Albert Wilson, Bill Brownson, Don Chell, Stan Weston.

Parwich Football Club in the 1930s. **Back row from left:** G. Brownson, S. Flower, T. Flower, C. Webster, T. Adams, W. Wayne (chairman). **Second from back:** W. Lees, O. Twigge, A. Gibbs (secretary). **Third from back:** F. Lees, F. Calladine, B. Twigge. **Front row:** D. Calladine (?), H. Lowndes, G. Blackwell, G. Flowers.

Parwich Football Team with the cups they won in the 1950 season.

Parwich Football Club 1951-52. **Back row from left:** L. Chadwick (trainer), C. Lowndes, D. Wayne, T. Spencer, F. Steeples, E. Tomlinson, J. Hobson, F. Calladine (chairman). **Front row:** L. Gibbs, A. Wilson, S. Wilson, P. Johnson, D. Chell, J. Lees (manager).

Parwich Football Team.

Ladies Football team, in the 1960s. Includes Christine Weston, Shirley Gibbs, Jean Calladine, Hazel Calladine, Veronica Twigge and Carol Cooper. There was a Ladies Football team in Parwich at one time, but there is some disagreement as to whether the group above is that team or a part of the Wakes Week Carnival.

The Darts Team. **Back row from left:** Don Wayne, Arthur Wayne, Frank Lees, Harold Gibbs, Frank Steeples, ?. **Front row:** ?, Ron Twigge, Ted Fearn, Albert Wilson, Sid Poyser.

Parwich Cricket Team. **Back row from left:** Harry Twigge (the one eyed umpire), Peter Rawlins, Ronny Calladine, ?, Abel Shipley, ? Johnson. **Front row:** Frank Johnson, ? Rogers, Clarence Weston, John Kirkham, Arthur Wayne, Geoffery Twigge.

Dennis Smith, the Derbyshire and England opening bat, speaking at the Parwich Cricket Club dinner held in the Sycamore Inn club room. From left: Mrs Henry Twigge, Sir John Crompton-Inglefield, Henry Twigge, Lady Crompton-Inglefield, Dennis Smith.

Above: Parwich Cricket Club Dinner. From left: ?, B. Brown, F. B. Hampson, G. Wayne.

Left: Sir John Crompton-Inglefield receiving a silver tankard from Harry Twigge for his twenty five years service to the Parwich Cricket Club as President and Chairman.

Abel Shipley receiving a cricket bat from Sir John Crompton- Inglefield.

The opening of the cricket pavilion by Stanley Thornton who donated it to the playing field.

Parwich Cricket Team pictured on the Uttoxeter race course whilst beating Uttoxeter 1st Eleven by 10 wickets. **Back row:** ??: Albert Kirkham, Cecil Twigge, Arthur Wayne, Frank Johnson, Len Johnson, Sam Wilson (Abel Shipley, Umpire). **Front Row:** Ron Calladine, John Kirkham (Capt.), Clarence Weston, Ian McConnochie, Albert Wilson.

Parwich Cricket team. **Back row from left:** Philip Allsopp, David Bacon, Simon Kirkham, Angus Smith, ?, David Swindell. **Front row:** Ray Stone, Stephen Rhodes, John Flower, Larry Bird, George McCabe, Stuart Chambers, Arthur Wayne.

Restarting the Cricket team in 1981.

The Parwich Kwik Cricket Team, July 2000. **Back, from left:** Alan Smith, Stephen Griffiths, David Swindell, Larry Birds. **Middle, from left:** Daniel Wood, James Slater, David Smith, Andrew Griffiths, Adam Swindell. **Front, from left:** Joel Day, Paul Williams, Nicholas Birds, Thomas Griffiths, Thomas Slater.

Parwich Tug of War Team. **Back row from left:** Andrew Knight, Arnold Chadfield, Philip Hancock, Peter Harris, Roger Cundy. **Front row:** Gary Hancock, Brian Foden, Brian McCormick.

Tug of War team with their trainer Eric Barker.

The Pikehall Tug of War Team.

Building the Bowling Green. From left: David Wigley, Brian Foden, Jim Wigley, George McCabe.

Mike Hart, president of the Bowling Club, presenting the trophies.

Left: Sir William Evans, first Chairman of the Derbyshire County Council 1889-1939. Of all those in Parwich's past, Sir William has had the greatest influence on the appearance of the village today, as it was he who financed the both the building of Parwich School and the rebuilding of St Peter's Church. He did not, however, live much in the village, although he owned Parwich Hall and its estate.

Below: The gardens of Parwich Hall sometime before 1911, when it was occupied by the Revd Claude Lewis who fell out so spectacularly with the village over arrangements for the celebration of the Coronation of George V that he eventually had to leave the village. It was the Lewis family that commissioned Walter Tapper to design the new wing for the Hall. The gardens were included in Tapper's brief, and for these he designed the five massive terraces seen here, which take the gardens up the side of Parwich Hill.

Left: The Gadsby sisters. The Gadsby sisters lived at the Fold and many views of Parwich survive thanks to their prolific postcard letter writing habit.

Right: The Fold. The two girls in the photo are, in all probability, the Gadsby sisters and the man to the right may be their uncle Wright Greatorex.

Left: The Gadsby sisters in the garden at the Fold, with their aunt Mrs Greatorex.

Above: John Burford. *Inset:* John Burford was constable at Parwich from May 1877 to February 1885. He returned to duty in Parwich from 1891 to 1893, having been promoted to Sergeant. He later went on to Derby as Superintendent and died in 1913 aged 58.

Above: John Burford's funeral in Ashbourne.

Left: Martha Maria Burford, wife of John Burford, 1850 – 1904. She was known for her kindness to the inmates of the lockup of which John Burford was in charge. It was said in her obituary that many of these would come to thank her after their release. There was a lock-up in Parwich (and, at one point, stocks on the village green) but its location is unknown.

Left: John William Burford, son of John Burford. He was Registrar of Births, Marriages and Deaths for Parwich and the surrounding area for over 40 years and died in 1963 at the age of 82.

Below: Florence Lillian (née Arnold), wife of John William Burford.

Right: John William Burford was very fond of pigeon racing and was the founding member of the Ashbourne Flying Club. During the First World War, he was assigned to the Pigeon Corps.

Below: The Burfords raised their eight children in Elm Cottage, pictured here at their parents' Golden Wedding Anniversary. **From left:** Peggy, Val, Phyllis, Eric, Vera, Jim, Sybil and Enid.

Walter and Millicent Wayne outside Church Farm on their wedding day. They later became landlord and lady of the Sycamore Inn.

Violet and Rosa Annie Allsop of circa 1900. The Allsop family name is said to be the oldest name in the village. All the Allsop and Allsopps (the spelling of the name varies, even within the family) in the village are descended from Sampson Allsop who came here from Alsop Moor and married Jeanetta Katherine Brownlee in 1885. They had seven children, of whom Violet and Rosa were the youngest.

The four daughters of Jeanetta and Sampson Allsop. **From left:** Lily, Violet, Fanny and Rosa Allsop, July 1916.

Right: Jeanetta Allsop with her daughter Lily and granddaughter Daisy Schofield (née Allsop).

Left: Walter Davey Schofield and Lily (née Allsopp), 1918.

Below: Violet Allsopp.

Above: Rosa Annie Allsopp.

Above: Jeanetta Allsopp (right).

Right: Fay Schofield (daughter of Lily and Walter Schofield) and Cecil Hardy (husband of Fanny Allsop) 1926.

Below: Jeanetta Allsopp and her grandson (Rosa Annie's son) Cecil Twigge.

Left: James Brownson was a well to do valuer and auctioneer. He gave Parwich the village pump – which continued in use until recently, sheltered by the Hampson Memorial. He may have lived at Hallcliffe, which belonged to his father in 1881. He also owned Brentwood, which he rented to his son James.

Right: James with his great grandchild.

Poster advertising one of James Brownson's auctions. Lot 1 is shown as being occupied by John Prince, who would later be the landlord of the Crown Inn until 1915.

George and Esther Brownson were married in 1904 in Huddersfield. George had grown up in Parwich and it was there they decided to return when their baby Muriel failed to thrive in the city air.

Brentwood around 1900 before the shop was added. This cottage was owned by James Brownson at the time and in 1907 it became the home of his son George who moved here with his wife and their daughter Muriel. A shop was built onto the house at this time and it was run as a general store by Esther and her sister Annie. George made picture frames in a workshop at the back of the shop. Although this photo was taken around the same time, the man standing by the gate is almost certainly not George Brownson as he would never have allowed himself to be photographed in the street.

Left: Mary Ann Shaw, mother of Esther Brownson. She had lived in Huddersfield all her life, but came to Parwich in 1927 at the age of 86 to live with her daughter.

Below: Muriel Brownson with Mary Anne Shaw outside Brentwood. As a child, Muriel attended not the village school, but a school for 'daughters of gentlemen' in Ashbourne. Getting there involved a two mile walk over the hill to the Bletch and then over field and hill to the Tissington station to board the train to Ashbourne.

Esther devoted much time to the local Red Cross during the Second World War. She led a work group which produced over a thousand garments for the troops. For this, she received a citation and a medal after the war. This photograph is said to have appeared in the Tatler.

George in his garden at Brentwood around 1925.

Above: Muriel Brownson's
wedding. Dolly Bunting
and Alice Twigge were
bridesmaids.

Left: Muriel Brownson.

Annie Shaw in the back garden of Brentwood.

Jim Hopkins outside his home Walnut Cottage. In younger years, he was a gardener for Mary Brownson (who is remembered for the peacocks in her garden) at Townhead. Esther Brownson stands in the doorway.

Henrietta Rawlins,
housemaid at Parwich Hall.

William George Rawlins.
Chauffeur at Parwich Hall.

The Crompton-Inglefields came to Parwich in 1931. **Back:** John Crompton-Inglefield, Gilbert Inglefield (later Lord Mayor of London). **Second from back:** Rosemary, Patricia, Isma, Mrs Gilbert Inglefield. **Third from back:** Caroline, Lady Crompton-Inglefield, child of Mr & Mrs Gilbert Inglefield. Front: child of Mr & Mrs Gilbert Inglefield.

Rosemary Crompton-Inglefield with her three daughters, Patricia (Bagshawe), Isma (Lutyens) and Caroline (Kilner) in the garden of Parwich Hall, circa 1938 – 1939.

Left: Harry Hopkinson, Head Gardener at the Hall in the 1960s, with trophies for his chrysanthemums – probably from the Mayfield Show.

Below: The gardens of Parwich Hall, when Harry Hopkinson was in charge.

Sir John Crompton-Inglefield's 80th birthday, at the house of his daughter Isma in Hampshire, with the people from Parwich who used to work for him. **From left:** Isma Lutyens, Cecil Twigge, Mrs Cecil Twigge, Sir John-Crompton Inglefield, Jack Cundy (estate joiner), Hetty Rawlins (maid), Vera Cundy, Mr Wingfield (butler), Betty Wain, Mrs Hopkinson, Mr Hopkinson (gardener).

Presentation of a picture of Parwich village to Sir John Crompton-Inglefield. **Back row from left:** Clem Edge, Chris Read, Alan Oldfield, Mrs Kirkham, Mrs Wheeldon, Mr Slater. **Front row:** Mrs Ratcliffe, Cath Goldstraw, Lady Crompton-Inglefield, Sir John Crompton-Inglefield, Anne Slater, Mrs Slater.

Donald Shields who purchased the Hall from the Crompton-Inglefields in 1976
and is the present owner of the Hall.

A Garden Fete at Parwich Hall to raise funds for the Parwich Hospital Trust. Donald and Rosemary Shields played a major role in getting the funds needed to buy the Rathborne Hospital back from the NHS, and enlisted the help of the M.P. Matthew Parris and the actor Alan Bates to publicise the cause. Although the NHS had originally bought the building for £1 it was sold to the Parwich Hospital Trust for £115,000. The Trust also raised the funds for the extensive work needed to convert the Hospital for use as a home for the elderly. **From left:** Mrs D. Roffe, Donald and Rosemary Shields, Nicky Clews, Sister Stafford, Penny Chettle, Mrs Leeds, ?.

Robert and Alice Shields, the present occupants of Parwich Hall, and their
children John, Elizabeth, Emma, Eleanor and David.

Ella Hopkinson with village children. **From left:** Reg Twigge, John Appleby, Eric Allsopp, John Hopkinson, Phyllis Allsopp, Jill Ridgard, Daniel Hopkinson. Ella was working as a nanny for the children of the Rothschild family when she met Harry, who was working at the time as a gardener for Lord Rothschild's mother at Ashton Wold. They settled in Parwich when Harry came here to work as a gardener at Parwich Hall.

Ella Hopkinson with friends at the Cake Stall during a garden fete at the Hall.
From left: Ella, Mrs Fearn (school caretaker), Mrs Lees.

Above: Marriage of Vernon and Annie Wibberley. **Back:** Dennis Wibberley, Jack Sims. **Middle:** Eileen James, Vernon Wibberley, Annie, Jessie Wibberley. **Front:** Barbara Webster, Maureen James.

Left: Vernon and Annie Wibberley outside Westview cottages. They were the first inhabitants of their cottage and remained there for many years.

Peter Rawlins in the military police 1953 – 55.

Frank Steeples with Karen Steeples and pony.

Anne and Jack Cooper with Hugh Gibson, when Jack Cooper was vicar of Parwich.

Anne Cooper and her farewell card from Parwich School.

Tom Sims receiving an award for 50 years service at Friden Brickworks.

Left: Iris Lowndes with her daughter Linda and their pet fox. On one occasion, her husband Don decided that the fox should be returned to the wild. He drove it out into the countryside and set it free, only to find the fox waiting for him on the doorstep when he got home!

Below: Linda Lowndes with a choice of transport!

Tea at the Memorial Hall. **From left:** Cath Goldstraw, Marjorie Twigge, Blanche Robotham, Anne Knight and Ruby Hickmott.

Right: Easter Egg hunt at the vicarage in 1997. **From left:** John Gordon, Lisa Wood, James Taylor, ?, ?, Mark Bainbridge, Daniel Wood, Mark Harrison, Sally Gordon. **Front:** Peter Harrison.

Left: The Parwich Mystery Child. This card belongs to Joyce Fortune and came from the Prince family which once ran the Crown Inn. The card comes from the same source as that which produced the village photo postcard at the end of this chapter. The reverse reads, in adult hand, "Wishing you a very happy Christmas for (sic) Sister Lizzie Ann for dear Ethel." I have not found anyone who can identify the child or the doorway she is standing in.

Children enjoying a steam train ride in the grounds of Parwich Hall during a Church Fete in 1998. **From left:** ?, Emma Shields, Mark Harrison, David Shields and Peter Harrison.

An early group photo of the village.

The village in 1992. An attempt was made to take another such photo in 2002 to commemorate the Queen's Golden Jubilee, but due to various misunderstandings and bad weather, not all the villagers were present on that occasion.

Celebration for the coronation of George V in 1911. The Coronation Committee.

Coronation of George V. The Village wanted to use the school premises for the celebrations, but the Lewis family still owned the school and the Revd Claude Lewis refused to grant permission for its use. The subsequent row led to Claude Lewis being burnt in effigy on the Church Green within view of the church door. The Lewis family left soon after and moved to Wales, claiming that the Derbyshire weather did not agree with Mrs Lewis.

Left and below: Fred Moorcroft. Sgt. Fred Moorcroft of the Sherwood Foresters was killed on 3rd of January 1918 and is buried at the Philosophie British Cemetery, Mazingarbe.

In the gardens of Parwich Hall, celebrating the end of the war in 1918.

Above: The Red Cross nurses at the Rathborne Hospital with Dr Hollick, the local G.P., in 1945-7. Cath Goldstraw is at the far left.

Left: Harry Hopkinson: Royal Marines Signals, 1941 – 45. Ella Hopkinson: Civil Nursing Auxiliary, 1943 – 45.

Thomas Keeling – Home Guard, Parwich.

There were Land Girls in Parwich during the war. Perhaps these are some of them?

Mary Keeling (Rawlins) with her father Thomas Keeling and two Italian prisoners of war from the POW camp at Biggin. They were sent to work at Upper Moor Farm, and here they are harvesting turnips.

William Mace: Grenadier Guards 1935 – 1944.
He was killed at Bayeaux in 1944, aged 32.

Nigel Mace: Infantryman, 1st Royal
Warwickshires 1960 – 67. Son of William Mace.

Left: Alan Oldfield was posted to Germany after the war in 1950. Aged 19, he was stationed opposite the former concentration camp of Belsen and experienced close up the horrors of the aftermath of the war.

Below: On manoeuvres in Germany.

Left and below: Upper Moor Farm during the snows of 1947. Children were off school for 8 weeks as the villages were cut off by the snow. The only way to get water to the cattle was to melt snow on the kitchen range. Milk could not be got away from the farm during this time, so they made it into butter which they sold, along with milk, by the side of the Buxton Road. 100 Council men with shovels came to unblock the road up to the Buxton Road, but they hardly had done the job before the wind came and blew all the snow back.

Left: Snows of 1947. A 15ft snowdrift blocked the Thorns Lane entrance to the village. Trees had to be cut down and the wood used as fuel. Food, already short because of wartime rationing, became very scarce. (H. Birkentall)

Celebrating the 50th anniversary of V. E. Day in 1995.

V. E. anniversary celebrations with Parwich Legion and Girl Guides.

Left: Street Party outside the Sycamore, for the V. E. Day anniversary.

Below: V. E. Day anniversary celebrations. **From left:** Denis Laycock, David Woolley, Roy Milward, Rob Francis, ?, Ben Laycock, Brian McCormick.

Candlelit procession to mark the Queen's Silver Jubilee. **Clockwise from left, excluding two children in lower left corner:** Peter Evans, Alan Oldfield, Jonathan Foden, Belinda Lowes, Janet Twigge, James Bunting, Karen Watson, Paul Watson, Janice Wigley, Peggy Lees (?), John Lees, Dorothy Foden, Tom Coleman, Alan Lowes, Shirley Bradbury, Val Kirkham, Margaret Lynam.

In June 2002 a bonfire was lit on Parwich Hill as part of the Jubilee chain of beacons celebrating the Queen's Golden Jubilee. Watching the fire is the Revd Christopher Harrison and beside him is the Bishop of Patna, Bishop Philip Marandih who was visiting Parwich at the time.

"The first motorcar to run through Parwich caused an amusing rush into the streets. What was not so amusing was the terrified rearing of the horses when they met the first petrol driven engine". (H.Birkentall)

Early camping holiday. It is not clear whether this wonderful car and caravan was owned by a Parwich resident or whether the occupants are visiting.

Above: The Northwestern bus ran until 1956 on the A515. It ran every two hours and was the only transport available for many.

Left: Of course the motor car eventually began to appear in Parwich as it did everywhere else, but in the early days it was a novelty and many photos were taken by the proud owners.

Though the bicycle has always been a useful form of transport in this area,
it is less used these days by locals.

Don Lowndes indulging his passion for sports cars!

THE "TELEGRAPH" RAILWAY TIME TABL[E]

EUSTON, ASHBOURNE, BUXTON AND MANCHESTER (L, & N.W.)

WEEK DAY.	a.m.	a.m.	a.m.	p.m.	p.m.	p.m. Sunda[y]
EUSTON, dep.	...	...	10 37	...	...	5 30
Nuneaton	...	...	12 55	...	...	7 25
Burton	...	...	1 53	...	...	8 17
Uttoxeter	...	...	2 19	...	...	8 37
ASHBOURNE	...	...	2 48	...	...	9 7
" dep	7 10	10 50	2 50	4 15	7 50	9 9
Thorpe Cloud	7 18	10 58	2 58	4 24	7 59	9 17
Tissington	7 22	11 4	3 3	4 30	8 6	9 22
Alsop-en-le-dale	7 30	11 11	3 9	4 37	8 18	9 28
Hartington	7 42	11 23	3 19	4 47	8 27	9 38
Parsley Hay	7 49	11 30	...	4 54	8 36	...
Hurdlow	7 55	11 35	...	4 59	8 41	...
Hindlow	8 2	11 41	3 y 30	5 4	8 48	...
H'r Buxt'n	8 8	11 47	...	5 13	...	...
BUXTON ar.	8 12	11 50	3 37	5 16	8 57	9 55
Dove Holes	8 25	1 57	...	5 42	9 32	10 y32
Chapel-en-le-Frth	8 35	1 33	...	5 48	9 39	10 y38
Whaley Bridge	8 45	1 40	...	5 55	9 47	10 y45
New Mills	9 3	1 48	...	6 3	9 55	10 y50
Stockport	9 9	12 48	...	6 27	10 17	...
MANCHESTER	9 1	1 0	...	6 40	10 35	...
MANCHESTER dep.	...	7 35	9 17	...	1 20	44 50
Stockport	...	7 47	9 27	...	1 31	44 59
New Mills	...	8 12	9 48	...	1 49	4 41
Whaley Bridge	...	8 22	9 55	...	1 55	4 49
Chapel-en-le-Frith	...	8 33	10 6	...	2 4	4 59
Dove Holes	...	8 40	10 12	...	2 11	5 6
BUXTON dep ...	7 50	9 0	10 30	12 45	2 27	5 50
Higher Buxton	...	9 3	10 33	...	2 30	5 53
Hindlow	...	9 12	10 42	...	2 39	6 2
Hurdlow	...	9 18	10 48	...	2 45	6 8
Parsley Hay	...	9 26	10 57	...	2 54	6 15
Hartington	8 13	9 32	11 4	1 7	3 0	6 21
Alsop-en-le-Dale	8 22	9 40	11 13	1 15	3 8	6 30
Tissington	8 26	9 45	11 21	1 20	3 15	6 42
Thorpe Cloud	8 33	9 49	11 25	1 23	3 19	6 52
ASHBOURNE dep.	8 38	9 54	11 30	1 28	3 25	7 0
" dep	8 41	...	...	1 34	...	...
Uttoxeter	9 9	...	...	2 2	...	...
Burton	9 44	...	...	2 31	...	...
Nuneaton	10 28	...	...	3 12	...	...
EUSTON, arr.	12 25	...	...	5 40	...	...

The Alsop train station played a vital part in Parwich life for 55 years and many relied on the trains to get to town and to transport the milk from the farms. The line was also much used by the local quarries. Regular passenger service came to an end in the mid 1950s and the line was finally closed and converted to a walking and bicycling trail in 1971.

Above: The Tissington station on the Buxton to Ashbourne line in 1952. Parwich residents would frequently walk over the hill to Tissington to catch the train from this station.

A more traditional form of transport – Gypsies camping outside Parwich.

Chapter 13 – Alsop-en-le-Dale

Only two miles down the road from Parwich and very much smaller than its neighbour, Alsop-en-le-Dale nevertheless manages to preserve its very distinctive identity. The majority of its inhabitants are farmers or of farming families and it is a close knit and warm community.

Alsop-en-le-Dale from above.

Alsop Hall, opposite the church, was built by the Alsop family in the late 16th century. The Alsops owned the estate from the early 12th to the late 17th century.

Alsop Church before the addition of the square tower. This is an older church than St Peter's in Parwich, and round the doorway can be seen the marks left from sharpening arrows around the time of the Battle of Agincourt, when archery practice was compulsory for all men and boys on Sundays.

Interior of St Michael and All Angels Church, Alsop-en-le-Dale.

Below left: An episode of the Peak Practice series was filmed at Alsop Church in 1993. Seen here is the Revd Jack Cooper with the actor Kevin Whately. *Above:* Amanda Burton from Peak Practice.

Right: John Booth has been organist at Alsop Church for many years.

Above: Tom Bunting, Clem Edge and William Bunting. Ringing the bell at Alsop Church.

Left: One of William Bunting's Friesians from Cross Low Bank in Alsop-en-le-Dale.

Below: William Bunting's Friesian herd.

Clem Edge at the Hartington Wakes.

Dry stone walling competition at Friden, just outside Alsop-en-le-Dale in 1937. There were many such competitions at the time and Clem Edge competed in this one in the under 18s division. An adult competitor was expected to lay a rood (7 yards) of drystone wall – which was considered the amount a skilled workman could lay in a day. These competitions came to an end at the beginning of the Second World War.

Three generations of William Buntings - the 2001 silage team.

Four young Alsop handlers and their awards. **At left, standing:** William Bunting, Andrew Bradbury. **At left, kneeling:** Daniel Bradbury. **Second from right:** standing, Anna Bunting.

Left, William Bunting with his reserve champion calf Alsop dale Larissa 7, in August 1998.

Toll Bar Cottage, New Inns, in the snows of 1947.

Alsop in the snows of 1947.